Adult and Baby Animals

WRITTEN BY

Kelly Ward

Published by Inhabit Education | www.inhabiteducation.com

Inhabit Education (Iqaluit), P.O. Box 2129, Iqaluit, Nunavut, X0A 1H0
(Toronto), 191 Eglinton Avenue East, Suite 302, Toronto, Ontario, M4P 1K1

Printed in Canada.

ISBN: 978-1-77266-083-8

This is a polar bear and its cub.

This is a wolf and its pup.

This is a beluga and its calf.

This is a walrus and its pup.

This is a Canada goose and its gosling.

This is a snowy owl and its owlet.

This is a muskox and its calf.